D1090881

Full **STEAM** Ahead!

Engineering Everywhere

How Engineers Solve Problems

Robin Johnson

CRABTREE
PUBLISHING COMPANY
WWW.CRABTREEBOOKS.COM

Title-Specific Learning Objectives:

Readers will:

- Identify and describe the steps of the engineering design process.
- Explain how the engineering design process helps engineers solve problems and meet needs effectively.
- Identify and restate main ideas in the text.

High-frequency words (grade one)	Academic vocabulary
a, and, are, as, for, like, made, many, that, to, use	creative, diagram, engineering design process, imagine, improve, model, plan, solution, solve, technologies

Before, During, and After Reading Prompts:

Activate Prior Knowledge and Make Predictions:

Have children read the title and look at the cover and title-page images. Ask:

- What do you know about engineers?
- What kinds of problems do you think engineers solve? What problem might the engineers in the images on the cover and title page be solving?
- Are you a problem solver?

During Reading:

After reading each page (10 to 18) that outlines the steps in the engineering design process, ask children:

- What is the main idea on this page?

- Can you explain the main idea in your own words?
- How is this step an important part of the engineering design process?
- How does this step connect with the step before it? Can you predict which steps might come next?

After Reading:

Make an anchor chart with the steps of the engineering design process. Ask children to explain each step in their own words, and write down child-friendly definitions for each step.

Have a group discussion about why it is important to learn from mistakes and repeat the process again and again until the solution works.

Author: Robin Johnson

Series Development: Reagan Miller

Editor: Janine Deschenes

Proofreader: Melissa Boyce

STEAM Notes for Educators: Reagan Miller and Janine Deschenes

Guided Reading Leveling: Publishing Solutions Group

Cover, Interior Design, and Prepress: Samara Parent

Photo research: Samara Parent

Production coordinator: Katherine Berti

Photographs:

Alamy: Westend61 GmbH: p. 17
Shutterstock: waller66: p. 7 (bottom right); John_Silver: p. 13 (bottom left)
All other photographs by Shutterstock

Library and Archives Canada Cataloguing in Publication

Title: How engineers solve problems / Robin Johnson.
Names: Johnson, Robin (Robin R.), author.
Description: Series statement: Full STEAM ahead! | Includes index.
Identifiers: Canadiana (print) 20189061863 |
  Canadiana (ebook) 20189061871 |
  ISBN 9780778762065 (hardcover) |
  ISBN 9780778762515 (softcover) |
  ISBN 9781427122629 (HTML)
Subjects: LCSH: Engineering—Juvenile literature. | LCSH: Engineers—Juvenile literature. | LCSH: Problem solving—Juvenile literature.
Classification: LCC TA149 .J645 2019 | DDC j620—dc23

Library of Congress Cataloging-in-Publication Data

Names: Johnson, Robin (Robin R.), author.
Title: How engineers solve problems / Robin Johnson.
Description: New York, New York : Crabtree Publishing Company, [2019] | Series: Full STEAM ahead! | Includes index.
Identifiers: LCCN 2018056592 (print) | LCCN 2018059402 (ebook) |
  ISBN 9781427122629 (Electronic) |
  ISBN 9780778762065 (hardcover : alk. paper) |
  ISBN 9780778762515 (pbk. : alk. paper)
Subjects: LCSH: Engineering--Juvenile literature. | Problem solving--Juvenile literature.
Classification: LCC TA149 (ebook) | LCC TA149 .J639 2019 (print) | DDC 620--dc23
LC record available at https://lccn.loc.gov/2018056592

Printed in the U.S.A./042019/CG20190215

Table of Contents

Crabtree Publishing Company

www.crabtreebooks.com   1-800-387-7650

Copyright © **2019 CRABTREE PUBLISHING COMPANY**. All rights reserved. No part of this publication may be reproduced, stored in a retrieval system or be transmitted in any form or by any means, electronic, mechanical, photocopying, recording, or otherwise, without the prior written permission of Crabtree Publishing Company. In Canada: We acknowledge the financial support of the Government of Canada through the Book Publishing Industry Development Program (BPIDP) for our publishing activities.

Published in Canada
Crabtree Publishing
616 Welland Ave.
St. Catharines, Ontario
L2M 5V6

Published in the United States
Crabtree Publishing
PMB 59051
350 Fifth Avenue, 59th Floor
New York, New York 10118

Published in the United Kingdom
Crabtree Publishing
Maritime House
Basin Road North, Hove
BN41 1WR

Published in Australia
Crabtree Publishing
Unit 3 – 5 Currumbin Court
Capalaba
QLD 4157

Who are Engineers?

Engineers are people who use math, science, and **creative thinking** to solve problems.

Engineers solve many different kinds of problems.
They find solutions that keep us safe, such as helmets.
They find solutions that make life easier, such as computers.

An umbrella is a solution that keeps us dry on rainy days.

Engineers work together to find solutions.

By Design

Engineers **design** things that solve problems. The things they design are called **technologies**.

Engineers design ways for people who live far apart to talk to each other.

Engineers **improve** technologies. They make them work better.

An engineer named Alexander Graham Bell made the first telephone. Engineers have improved telephones over time.

Following Steps

Engineers follow steps to solve problems. The steps are called the engineering design **process**.

Ask

Imagine

Plan

Create

Improve

These are the steps of the engineering design process. Keep reading to learn about each step.

Engineers do not always get their designs
right the first time. They learn from mistakes.
They follow the steps again and again to improve.

Ask!

First, engineers ask questions. They ask what the problem is. They ask how other people have tried to solve it. They ask what challenges they might face in solving the problem.

Asking questions helps engineers find the best way to solve a problem.

An engineer might ask how to design a taller building.

An engineer might ask how to get **energy** from the wind.

💡 Imagine!

Next, engineers **imagine** as many solutions as they can. They work in groups to think of many solutions. Then, they choose the best solution to the problem.

During this step of the process, engineers brainstorm to find solutions. To brainstorm means to talk and come up with ideas in a group.

Engineers imagined ways for people to travel to space. They decided the best solution was a rocket.

Plan!

The third step is to plan the design. Engineers draw a diagram of their best solution.

Diagrams are drawings that show the parts of an object, and how it works.

Engineers make a list of the materials they will need. Materials are the things an object is made of.

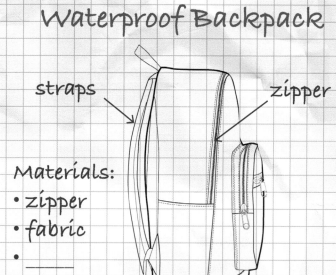

Waterproof Backpack

straps

zipper

Materials:
- zipper
- fabric
- ___
- ___

These engineers are making a plan to design a waterproof backpack. They drew a diagram of the backpack. They are making a list of materials they will need.

Create!

Next, engineers create, or make, a **model** of their solution. They follow their plan to make the model.

Models can be objects or drawings.

Engineers use models to test their solutions. They test their solutions to find out if they work. They write down if the solution solved the problem.

This engineer is using a model to test the design of his robot. He writes down the parts that work. He writes down the parts that do not work.

Improve!

After they test their solution, engineers see how well it solved the problem. Then, they improve the design. They change it to make it work better.

The tests help engineers learn what doesn't work well. Then, they fix the mistakes and improve their design.

18

Engineers improve and test their solutions again and again to make sure they solve the problem.

Engineers test seat belts to make sure they will keep people safe in a car crash. They improve the seat belts to make sure they work well.

Do It Again

Solving problems is not easy! Engineers often repeat steps in the process again and again, until their solution works well.

Engineers work together to improve their designs.
They keep trying until they find a solution that works well.

You can work together and solve problems like engineers!

Words to Know

creative thinking [kree-EY-tiv THING-king] noun Using your mind to make up new and original ideas

design [dih-ZAHYN] verb To make a plan for how something is made or built

energy [EN-er-jee] noun The power to do work

imagine [ih-MAJ-in] verb To make an image of something in your mind

improve [im-PROOV] verb To make better

model [MOD-l] noun A representation or copy of a real object

process [PROS-es] noun Ongoing set of actions or changes

technologies [tek-NOL-uh-jees] noun Things people make to solve problems or meet needs

A noun is a person, place, or thing.

A verb is an action word that tells you what someone or something does.

An adjective is a word that tells you what something is like.

Index

About the Author

Robin Johnson is a freelance author and editor who has written more than 80 children's books. When she isn't working, Robin builds castles in the sky with her engineer husband and their two best creations—sons Jeremy and Drew.

To explore and learn more, enter the code at the Crabtree Plus website below.

www.crabtreeplus.com/fullsteamahead

Your code is:
fsa20

STEAM Notes for Educators

Full STEAM Ahead is a literacy series that helps readers build vocabulary, fluency, and comprehension while learning about big ideas in STEAM subjects. *How Engineers Solve Problems* helps readers identify and explain the main ideas of the engineering design process. The STEAM activity below helps readers extend the ideas in the book to build their skills in science, technology, and engineering.

Designing a Solution

Children will be able to:
- Use the engineering design process to create a solution that helps them reduce their impact on the local environment.

Materials
- Model Planning and Testing Sheet
- Engineering Design Process Worksheet
- Materials for project, including boxes, paper, cardboard, glue, tape, craft sticks, paper rolls, and art materials

Guiding Prompts
After reading *How Engineers Solve Problems*, ask:
- What is the engineering design process? Why is it useful for engineers?
- Can you describe each step of the process in your own words?

Activity Prompts
Review the steps of the engineering design process with children. It is useful if the steps are on an anchor chart for quick reference.

Explain to children that they will use the engineering design process to create a solution in their classroom (or in their home). Educator can choose any solution that fits with class interest and educational initiatives. Suggested problem to solve: Design a solution that reduces the amount of waste we create in our classroom (or at home).
- Review appropriate background context for the problem.

Hand each child an Engineering Design Process Worksheet. Complete the brainstorm stage together. Create a list of possible solutions that are realistic.

In groups of three to four, have children choose one solution from the list. They will follow the rest of the steps in the process to create a model and final version of the solution. They can use the Model Planning and Testing Sheet to help. Be sure to guide students throughout the process and allocate specific days for each step. Have children present their finished solutions.

Extensions
- Invite children to consider how they could adapt their solutions for a new purpose or location, such as reducing waste at a park.

To view and download the worksheets, visit **www.crabtreebooks.com/resources/ printables** or **www.crabtreeplus.com/ fullsteamahead** and enter the code **fsa20**.